The Eagle's Mile

Other books by James Dickey

James Dickey

The Eagle's Mile

Wesleyan University Press
Published by
University Press of New England
Hanover and London

The University Press of New England is a consortium of universities in New England dedicated to publishing scholarly and trade works by authors from member campuses and elsewhere. The New England imprint signifies uniform standards for publication excellence maintained without exception by the consortium members. A joint imprint of the University Press of New England and a sponsoring member acknowledges the publishing mission of that university and its support for the dissemination of scholarship throughout the world. Cited by the American Council of Learned Societies as a model to be followed, University Press of New England publishes books under its own imprint and the imprints of Brandeis University, Brown University, Clark University, University of Connecticut, Dartmouth College, University of New Hampshire, University of Rhode Island, Tufts University, University of Vermont, and Wesleyan University.

Some of these poems appeared previously in the following publications: *The Amicus Journal, Charleston Magazine, False Youth* (Pressworks Publishing, Inc.), *Harpers, Hastings Constitutional Law Quarterly, Head-Deep in Strange Sounds: Free Flight Improvisations from the Unenglish* (Palaemon Press, Ltd.), *Kenyon Review, Night Hurdling* (Bruccoli Clark, Inc.), *Paris Review, Proceedings, Southern Magazine, Southport, Värmland* (Palaemon Press, Ltd.), and *Verse*. "Gila Bend," "The Little More," and "The Six" first appeared in *Poetry*; "Basics: (I) Level, (II) Simplex," "Craters," "Eagles," "Expanses," "Farmers," "Moon Flock," "Night Bird," "Sleepers," "Snow Thickets," "Sea," "The One," "The Three," and "Weeds" first appeared in *The American Poetry Review*.

Printed in the United States of America

∞

Library of Congress Cataloging-in-Publication Data
Dickey, James.
The eagle's mile / James Dickey.
p. cm.
ISBN 0-8195-2185-X (alk. paper)—
ISBN 0-8195-1187-0 (alk. paper : pbk.)
I. Title.
PS3554.I32E34 1990
811'.54—dc20   89-49257
CIP

Wesleyan Poetry

5   4   3   2   1

To Deborah, my wife,
and to Chris, Kevin, Bronwen, James IV and Katie
. . . those of the blood, and the heart's-blood

Contents

Double-tongue:
Collaborations and Rewrites

The Eagle's Mile

Eagles

If I told you I used to know the circular truth

Of the void,
                 that I have been all over it building
   My height
                     receiving overlook

And that my feathers were not
Of feather-make, but broke from a desire to drink
The rain before it falls
                    or as it is falling:

If I were to tell you that the rise of any free bird
Is better

          the larger the bird is,

And that I found myself one of these
Without surprise, you would understand

That this makes of air a thing that would be liberty
Enough for any world but this one,
And could see how I should have gone

Up and out of all

         all of it

On feathers glinting

Multitudinously as rain, as silica-sparks around
One form with wings, as it is hammered loose
From rock, at dead
Of classic light: that is, at dead

Of light.

Believe, too,
While you're at it, that the flight of eagles has
For use, long muscles steeped only
In escape,
                    and moves through
Clouds that will open to nothing

But if, where the bird leaves behind
All sympathy: leaves
The man who, for twenty lines
Of a new poem, thought he would not be shut
From those wings: believed

He could be going. I speak to you from where

I was shook off: I say again, shook
Like thís, the words I had
When I could not spread:

            When thát bird rose

Without my shoulders: Leave my unstretched weight,
                    My sympathy grovelling
In weeds and nothing, and go
                        up from the human down-
beat in my hand. Go up without anything

Of me in your wings, but remember me in your feet

As you fold them. The higher rock iś
The more it lives. Where you take hold, Í will take

Thát stand in my mind, rock bird alive with the spirit-
life of height,
                    on my down-thousands
Of fathoms, classic

Claw-stone, everything under.

Gila Bend

Where aerial gunnery was, you think at first a cadaver

On foot might get through

Forty years after. Shots of space pelter back

Off the dead bullets; walking, you should brand, brand
The ground but you don't: you leave

Not a thing moving on a sand mountain
Smashed flat by something that didn't know
What else to do.
                              This silver small-stone heat
No man can cross; no man could get

To his feet, even to rise face-out

Full-force from the grave, where the sun is down on hím

Alone, harder than resurrection

Is úp: down harder

                              harder

Much harder than that.

Circuit

Beaches; it is true: they go on   on
And on, but as they ram and pack, foreseeing

Around a curve, always   slow-going headlong

For the circle
                              swerving from water
But not really, their minds on a perfect connection, no matter
How long it takes. You can't be
On them without making the choice
To meet yourself no matter

How long. Don't be afraid;
It will come   will hit you

Straight out of the wind, on wings or not,
Where you have blanked yourself

Still with your feet. It may be raining

In twilight, a sensitive stripping
Of arrow-feathers, a lost trajectory struck
Stock-stilling through them,
                              or where you cannot tell
If the earth is green or red,

Basically, or if the rock with your feet on it

Has floated over the water. As for where you are standing

Nów, there are none of those things; there are only
In one shallow spray-pool   thís one

Strong horses circling. Stretch and tell me, Lord;
Let the place talk.

This may just be it.

Night Bird

Some beating in there

That has bunched, and backed
Up in it out of moonlight, and now
Is somewhere around. You are sure that like a curving grave

It must be able to fall
               and rise
                         and fall and that's
   Right, and rise
             on your left hand
                     or other

Or behind your back on one hand

You don't have and suddenly there is no limit

To what a man can get out of
His failure to see:
               this gleam

Of air down the nape of the neck, and in it everything
There is of flight
          and nothing else,
                  and it is

All right and all over you
From around
          as you are carried

In yourself and there is no way
To nothing-but-walk—

No way and a bidden flurry
And a half-you of air.

Daybreak

You sit here on solid sand banks trying to figure
What the difference is when you see
The sun and at the same time see the ocean
Has no choice: none, but to advance more or less
As it does:
                    waves
Which were, a moment ago, actual
Bodiless sounds that could have been airborne,
Now bring you nothing but face-off

After face-off, with only gravitational sprawls
Laid in amongst them. To those crests
Dying hard, you have nothing to say:
                          you cannot help it

If you emerge; it is not your fault. You show: you stare

Into the cancelling gullies, saved only by dreaming a future
Of walking forward, in which you can always go flat

Flat down where the shallows have fallen
Clear: where water is shucked of all wave-law:
Lies running: runs

In skylight, gradually cleaning, and you gaze straight into

The whole trembling forehead of yourself
Under you, and at your feet find your body

No different from cloud, among the other
See-through images, as you are flawingly
Thought of,
                  but purely, somewhere,

Somewhere in all thought.

Two Women

I

Alone here. Beach, drum out
What you want to say: a dolphin,
Sockets, sword-flats. Seething landscape of hilts, no limits are set

In you. Sand, sand,
Hear me out: Hear me out with wind
Going over, past
All sound but sand. Listen,

Clean vastness, I am alone here.
I should be, for I have
No mark.
Woman, because I don't love you,
Draw back the first

Of your feet, for the other will fall
After it, and keep on coming. Hold back

A little, your printed pursuit, your

Unstemming impurity.

II

Early light: light less
Than other light. Sandal without power
To mark sand. Softly,
Her hair downward-burning, she walks here, her foot-touch

The place itself,

Like sand-grains, unintended,

Born infinite.

Immortals

Earth

Always as it holds us in one place, the earth
Grows as it moves, exhaling
Its rooted joy. I stand in tracks
Where nothing starves. Vegetation, green blush,
You and I sail today
Through newly infinite
Space on this surfeited hillside. Complacency has its own force

Leafed-out with renewal. I cannot be anything
But alive, in a place as far

From the blank and the stark, as this.

Air

Air, much greater than the sea—
More basic, more human than the sea: all thát air
Is calm:
        unpeopled, wearing the high lucidity

Of vigil. Maybe one day the mere surface
Of the earth will feel you. But the air
You can never keep doesn't know
When it lived in your chest:

Mindless, nerveless, breathless,
The air glitters
All the outside, and keeps carrying

You from within.

Sea

Who told you that the sea said something,
Something toward the beaches?
Let it spread more, belligerent with light,
Saying one thing, resounding,

Up front for all of us!

To the Butterflies

—homage, Central America

Open windows; we always have them, háve
To have them. We widen

Them all, and butterflies come in, and come

To rest on our mirrors, breathing with their wings

Almost like light,
Or better, almost like flight,

And then leave. Others come,
Háve to come, and some of the time this happens
We are singing, trying hard,

But it comes out a croak
From dryness, and when we move it is like
Moving muscles of powder, but
Really no muscles are on us; they are all gone
Into sweat. Every light the hand turns on
Hurts the eyes, and there is nowhere on earth
That the heels of the feet
Are so hot, and they cannot be cooled.
I love to know nothing

Of the sun; I love to feel

That I float, forgotten,
with two warm rivers
That cannot touch me, on a stream come down
Between them from a mountain
Of frozen rain. We all have wanted,

Too long, not to have our tears,
Our salt-showing tears, dry before anyone
Can see them, dry
Before we can feel them,
Or find out what they really have
To do with grief. To say that I am not true
To fever is to say I am not
Loyal to my green country,

not true, not real

Myself,
so I say it in secret

In steam: Forgive me, butterflies:
I know you have to have
All this heat for your colors,
but you are breathless, too,
In spite of your breathing

Wings and God help me I must say it before I melt
Into the sugar-sick ground:
If we could do it

Without dimming the butterflies, we should find some way
To get on the good side of North: Yes North and enough

Cold: Yes cold

And snow! I've heard of it! Flakes lilting onto us!

Life light on the common grave

Shapeless with swelter! Every tongue of us out

To be new to that taste! Mountains of rain
Gone into feather-fall
Floating us out of it! But not dimming   not fading
The butterflies
                              or the hats and handkerchiefs.
Let the wings on our mirrors

In whatever falls

Keep breathing   Keep burning

                              and us, Lord, please—

And us in the dresses and shirts.

The One

No barometer but yellow
Forecast of wide fields that they give out
Themselves, giving out they stand
In total freedom,

And will stand and day is down all of it

On an ear of corn. One. The color one:
One, nearly transparent
With existence. The tree at the fence must be kept

Outside, between winds; let it wait. Its movement,

Any movement, is not

In the distillation. Block it there. Let everything bring it
To an all-time stop just short of new
Wind   just short
Of its leaves;
                its other leaves.

One.

Inside.

Yellow.

All others not.

One.

One.

The Three

I alone, solemn land

                  clear, clean land,

See your change, just as you give up part
Of your reality:
              a scythe-sighing flight of low birds
    Now being gone:
              I, oversouling for an instant

       With them,
              I alone
See you as more than you would have

      Bé seen, yourself:
              grassland,
Dark grassland, with three birds higher
Than those that have left.
              They are up there
With great power:
        so high they take this evening for good
    Into their force-lines. I alone move

Where the other birds were, the low ones,
    Still swaying in the unreal direction
    Flocking with them. They are gone

And will always be gone; even where they believe
    They were is disappearing. But thése three
    Have the height to power-line all

Land: land this clear. Any three birds hanging high enough
    From you trace the same paths
As strong horses circling
              for a man alone, born level-eyed

As a pasture, but like the land
Tilting, looking up.

This may be it, too.

The Six

When you think strong enough, you get something
You don't mean
And you dó: something prized-out,
Splintered, like a rock quarry going
Through you and over you
Like love, and past and on

Like love: whatever arms, legs, head,

Breastbone, whatever feet and hands you love most,
Most want to live
And die with, are given out as flying
Related rock; are charged
With the life that lives
By means of stone. The body of your lover tries to form and be

Those six stones. For some reason

They are hurtling, and if you meet them head-on
You will know something nobody means

But her. She is moving at the speed of light

Some place else, and though she passes
Through you like rock-salt, she is still six
And not one.

But neither is the rain
Single, blotting number and stone
With vibrancy; neither is the rain, I tell you,
Man riddled with rocks
And lust:

the rain putting out
Your wretched, sympathetic
Stone-jawed poetic head, its allotted
Fresh bodies falling as you stand

In amongst, falling and more
Than falling   falling more

Falling   now falling

More than now.

Weeds

Stars and grass
Have between them a connection I'd like to make
More of—find some way to bring them

To one level any way I can,
And put many weeds in amongst. O woman, now that I'm thinking,
Be iń there somewhere! Until now, of the things I made up
Only the weeds are any good: Between them,

Nondescript and tough, I peer,
The backs of my hands

At the sides of my face, parting the stringy stalks.
Tangible, distant woman, here the earth waits for you
With what it does not need
To guess: with what it truly has
In its hands. Through pigweed and sawgrass

Move; move sharply; move iń
Through anything,
                    and hurt, if you have to. Don't come down;

Come forward. A man loves you.

Spring-Shock

All bubbles travelling

In tubes, and being lights: up down and around
They were: blue, red and every man uncaught

And guilty. Prison-paleness
Over the street between strobes
Unfailingly. But no light
On top of anything moving, until
The last, one:
           one. Whoever it was switched it

Dead when he saw me. Winter; not dreamlike but a dream and cars
Of that. I took my stand where they were called
By absent law to stop, obstructedly raging

And I could not get in. All their windows
Were sealed and throbbing
With strobe, red and blue, red and blue

And go. One pulled out of the flight
Of others; pulled up and may have had back-road
Dust on it   red dust in a last shot
Of blue. A man in a cowboy hat rolled down

The window on my side. His voice
Was home-born Southern; Oklahoma, Texas,
Could have been. Manhandling my overcoat, I slid
In there with him. Central Park South, I said,
A war-safety zone; the St. Moritz.

He turned up

One of the streets with no lights. Into the seat
I settled; black buildings thickened
Around us, high tenements flattening
Into squares; warehouses now,

They were; maybe docks. I watched. No birds.
No trash-cans. The car died

Between two alley walls

And froze, and a voice at last, still
Out of Oklahoma, said "I want your money."
                                        We were present
In silence. A brought-on up-backward thock

Took place, and on the fresh blade
A light alive in the hand
New-born with spring-shock. It was mine
At sixty. "I want your car," I said.

The Eagle's Mile

for Justice William Douglas

The Emmet's Inch & Eagle's Mile
—Blake

Unwarned, catch into this
With everything you have:
 the trout streaming with all its quick
 In the strong curve   all things on all sides
 In motion   the soul strenuous
And still
 in time-flow as in water blowing
 Fresh and for a long time

 Downhill   something like air it is
 Also and it is dawn

 There in merciless look-down
 As though an eagle or Adam
In lightning, or both, were watching uncontrollably
For meat, among the leaves. Douglas, with you
The soul tries it one-eyed, half your sight left hanging in a river
 In England, long before you died,

 And now thát one, that and the new one
 Struck from death's instant—
 Lightning's: like mankind on impulse blind-
 siding God—true-up together and ride
 On silence, enraptured surveillance,

The eagle's mile. Catch into this, and broaden

 Into and over

The mountain rivers, over the leaf-tunnel path:

Appalachia, where the trail lies always hidden

Like prey, through the trembling south-north of the forest
Continent, from Springer Mountain to Maine,
And you may walk

Using   not surpassing

The trout's hoisted stand-off with the channel,
Or power-hang the same in the shattered nerves
Of lightning: like Adam find yourself splintering out
Somewhere on the eagle's mile, on peerless, barbaric distance
Clairvoyant with hunger,

Or can begin   can be   begin to be
What out-gentles, and may evade:
This second of the second year
Of death, it would be best for the living
If it were your impulse to step out of grass-bed sleep

As valuably   as cautiously

As a spike-buck, head humming with the first male split
Of the brain-bone, as it tunes to the forked twigs
Of the long trail

Where Douglas you once walked in a white shirt as a man
In the early fall, fire-breathing with oak-leaves,
Your patched tunnel-gaze exactly right
For the buried track,
                    the England-curved water strong
Far-off with your other sight, both fresh-waters marbling together

Supporting not surpassing

What flows   what balances

In it. Douglas, power-hang in it all now, for all
The whole thing is worth: catch without warning

Somewhere in the North Georgia creek like ghost-muscle tensing
Forever, or on the high grass-bed
Yellow of dawn, catch like a man stamp-printed by God-
shock, blue as the very foot
Of fire. Catch into the hunted
Horns of the buck, and thus into the deepest hearing—
Nerveless, all bone, bone-tuned
To leaves and twigs—with the grass drying wildly
When you woke   where you stood with all blades rising
Behind you, and stepped out
                                  possessing the trail,
The racked bramble on either side shining
Like a hornet, your death drawing life
From growth
              from flow, as in the gill-cleansing turn
Of the creek
              or from the fountain-twist
Of flight, that rounds you
Off, and shies you downwind
Side-faced, all-seeing with hunger,

And over this, steep and straight-up
In the eagle's mile
Let Adam, far from the closed smoke of mills
And blue as the foot
Of every flame, true-up with blind-side outflash
The once-more instantly
Wild world: over Brasstown Bald

Splinter uncontrollably whole.

Daughter

Hospital, and the fathers' room, where light
Won't look you in the eye. No emergency
But birth. I sit with the friend, and listen

To the unwounded clock. Indirectly glowing, he is grayer,
Unshaven as I. We are both old men
Or nearly. He is innocent. Yet:
What fathers are waiting to be born
But myself, whom the friend watches
With blessed directness? No other man but a worker

With an injured eyeball; his face had been there
When part of an engine flew up.
A tall nurse blotted with ink
And blood goes through. Something written
On her? Blood of my wife? A doctor with a blanket
Comes round a blind corner. "Who gets this little girl?"
I peer into wool: a creature
Somewhat strangely more than red. Dipped in fire.

No one speaks. The friend does not stir; he is innocent
Again: the child is between
Me and the man with one eye. We battle in the air,
Three-eyed, over the new-born. The doctor says,
"All right, now. Which one of you had a breech baby?"
All around I look: look at the possible
Wounded father. He may be losing: he opens his bad eye.
I half-close one of mine, hoping to win
Or help. Breech baby. I don't know. I tell my name.
Taking the doctor by his arms
Around her, the child of fire moves off. I would give one eye for her

Already. If she's not mine I'll steal her.
The doctor comes back. The friend stirs; both our beards
Quicken: the doctor is standing
Over me, saying, "This one's yours."

                              It is done: I set my feet
In Heavenly power, and get up. In place of plastic, manned rubber
                    And wrong light, I say wordlessly
                Roll, real God. Roll through us. I shake hands

              With the one-eyed man. He has not gained
        A child, but may get back his eye; I hope it will return
                By summer starlight.
                                    The child almost setting
          Its wool on fire, I hold it in the first and last power
            It came from: that goes on all the time
            There is, shunting the glacier, whirling
            Whole forests from their tops, moving

            Lava, the flowing stone: moving the hand
                Of anyone, ever. Child of fire,
        Look up. Look up as I lean and mumble you are part
        Of flowing stone: understand: you are part of the wave,
                  Of the glacier's irrevocable
        Millennial inch.
                          "This is the one," the friend repeats
                In his end-of-it daze, his beard gone
        Nearly silver, now, with honor, in the all-night night
              Of early morning. Godfather, I say

          To him: not father of God, but assistant
      Father to this one. All forests are moving, all waves,
              All lava and ice. I lean. I touch

            One finger. Real God, roll.

            Roll.

The Olympian

Los Angeles back-yarding in its blue-eyed waters
Of empty swim, by my tract-house of packaged hard-candy
I lay in wait with the sun
And celebrity beer
for the Olympian,
Now my oldest boy's junior
High school algebra teacher, who had brought back the black-magic gold
Of the East, down the fast lane,
Freewaying, superhuman with rubberized home-stretch,
The four hundred meters from Tokyo
To Balboa Boulevard, leaving in his wake
All over the earth, the Others, the nation-motley doom-striped ones,
Those heart-eating sprinters, those Losers.
With Olympia Beer I was warming

Warming up with the best chill waters
Of the West Coast, cascading never-ending
Down out of Washington State. Now is your moment of truth
With me at last, O Champion! for I had laid a course as strange
To him as to me. Steeplechase! I had always leapt into water
Feet first, and could get out
Faster than in. I was ready for the Big One:
For the Water Jump in the corner
Of the lax, purfled pool, under the cemented palm
Where at night the shrewd rat climbed
And rustled and ruled the brown fronds over the underlit
Blue oval, surveying Sepulveda,
And in its color and kind, suffered
World recognition.
With a slide-rule in his shirt-pocket,
His bullet-proof glasses drawing
Into points—competitive points—and fish-eye-lensing,
Crossflashing on my hogged, haggard grassplot
Of slapped-down, laid-back Sepulveda, just after he'd Won It All,
He came lankily, finely drawn
Onto my turf, where all the time I had been laying
For him, building my energy-starches,

My hilarious, pizza-fed fury. My career of fat
Lay in the speed-trap, in the buckets and tools of the game-plan,
The snarls of purified rope. Then dawned the strict gods of Sparta,
The free gods of Athens! O lungs of Pheidippides collapsing in a square
Of the delivered city! O hot, just-hurdlable gates
Of deck-chairs! Lounges! A measured universe
Of exhilarating laws! Here I had come   there I'd gone
Laying it down   confusing, staggering
The fast lane and the slow, on and over
And over recliners, sun-cots, cleaning-poles and beach-balls,
Foiled cans of rusty rat-poison   bowing, split casks
Of diatomaceous earth   corks spaced-out like California
On blue-and-white dacron cords   lost-and-found swim-fins
Unmatched and pigeon-toed   half-hearted air
In blazing rings   doughnuts and play rafts   dragons and elephants
Blown-up by mouth, now sighing most of life
Away   the lawful No-Running signs
Turned to the wall. And all the time, all the time,
Under the brown-browed, rose-ash glower
Of the smog-bank, the crows, long gone
Gray with the risen freeways, were thronging and hawing
To be Doves of Peace   to be turned
Loose, displaying and escaping, over the jolted crowds
Of Unimart, the rammed Victory Stand,
                                        and in the rose-ash
Of early dusk, we called our wives, gray as crows
In their golf-hats, to the secret Olympics, laid down in my laws
Within laws, where world champions, now mad with the moon
Of moonlighting, sold running shoes. This so, we insisted
On commercials, those all-comers'
Career-dreams of athletes: "We are brought to you by the Bringers of the Flame,
The double-dry double martini," those women said. "Get set!
Get set! You're being born
Again, in spite of everything!" James Bond and my smallest boy
Blazed with one cap-pistol together. We hove like whales from the line.

Twice around

We were going for, cursing and cruising like ghosts, over dog-food bowls,
Over sprinklers passed-out from their spin-off
Of rainbows and I was losing
But not badly, and even gained a little, coming out
Of the water-jump and over the jump-rope, and out of him or maybe
Me   surely me   burst a mindless deep
Belching blindsiding laugh down the backstretch
Of earth-kegs and dirty cleansing-tools that skinned the dust
From the under-blue, and for one unsettling moment left it
Blazing and mattering. I blazed I felt great I was a great
Plaster stadium-god   lagging   lolloping   hanging
In there with the best: was running pale and heavy
With cement-dust   from two wives running
Then coming around   coming back
Down the slow lane   lurching   lorry-swaying:
Now toward two wives making up for   —making
The gelatin-murmur of crowds, I pounded, wet and laboring,
And then, half a pool
Behind, went into the bell-lap.
                    I was holding my own
Back there, as we rounded
Past the stands   he a long first and I
A world-class second and counting
On my finish or something   Yes! My finish to come
From the home turf like an ascension   all-seeing
World-recognized   poison-proof   smoke-proof   time-proof
Out of the pool, a rat's climb grappling
Half-a-lap half-a-lap   still alive
In mid-stride, louring, lumbering, crow-hopping
Behind the athlete's unhurried
Slack, unearthly footling lope:
                    I stepped low and heavy
Over the last light rope, smashed water with my sole
Flat   climbed, lurched, legged it and duck-footed

For home   a good not shameful
Second   this was all right and everything
But no! My weave   my plan   the run
Of my knots had caught up with him   caught
Him where he lived
            —in his feet—
                        and he was down
In styrofoam, and on a bloated blessèd doughnut-ring
Of rubber rolled: the finish-line leapt   exploded
Into Reality, shot-through with deathless flame, crossed with white paper:
            Swam illicitly, aboundingly
Like wind-aided glory. With courage to do credit
To any rat, I cornered and turned
It on. He came back instantly, but instantly was not soon
Enough, for I charged past like a slow freight
All over the earth, and had got it
And gone   long gone   and burst

Through the living tissue: breasted and blanked
The Tape and can feel it

Bannering, still, on my chest
Like wing-span, that once was toilet-paper, torn epically
Where the true Olympian slurred
His foot and fell, and I felt my lungs collapsing in a square
Of the City, like Pheidippides dying of the sheer
Good of my news.
                        Far off, still rising at rose dusk
And night, free under the low-browed smoke, and grayer
Than any fake peace-bird,
Like a called crow I answer
Myself utterly, with a whole laugh   —that body-language one-world
One word of joy   —straight into the ruining tons
Of smoke that trash my head and doom it
And keep it recognized
                        in the age
And condition of my kind, and hear also, maybe not entirely

From myself, the Olympian's laugh
Coming from somewhere
Behind, blindsidedly, getting the point
At last, sighing like ghosts and like rubber, for fat
And luck, all over the earth, where that day and any and every
Day after it, devil hindmost and Goddamn it

To glory, I lumbered for gold.

The Little More

JBTD

I

But the little more: the little more
This boy will be, is hard
For me to talk of
But harder for him. Manhood is only a little more,
A little more time, a little more everything than he

Has on him now. He would know, if he could go forward
From where he puts down his ball,
His top, his willow spear,
                              that he will face into the air
Where the others his age will be breaking, or be
About to break,
                    and he will watch them grow pale
With the warnings of doctors,
And all their balloons, and parents and the other
                    Dead will be floating

Away from them, over the mountains.
                                    I would tell him

            This is where the quiet

Valley comes in, and the red creek
Where he will row with no other,
The water around each blade
Explosive, ablaze with his only initials,
            Joy set in the bending void
Between the oars
                        and swung,
As the last balloon disappears, needing
Color no more. Yes! This is when the far mountain

35

Will come to him, under his feet
Of its own wish
                        when he steps up

From water, and in the wind he will start
To hear the enormous resonance
Children cannot make out: of his own gigantic
Continuous stride over all ferocious rocks

That can be known.

II

From the ones who have grown all they can
Come and stop softly, boy,
On the strong side of the road

That the other side does not see. Then move.
Put your feet where you look,
and not

Where you look, and none of your tracks
Will pass off, but wander, and for you

Be fresh places, free and aggressive.

Boy who will always be glanced-at
and then fixed

In warm gazes, already the past knows
It cannot invent you again,

For the glitter on top of the current
Is not the current.
No, but what dances on it is
More beautiful than what takes its time
Beneath, running on a single unreleased
Eternal breath, rammed
With carry, its all-out dream and dread

Surging bull-breasted,
Head-down, unblocked.

For a Time and Place
A South Carolina inauguration of Richard Riley as governor

May we be able to begin with ourselves
Underfoot and rising,
Peering through leaves we have basketed, through tendrils hanging
Like bait, through flowers,
Through lifted grave-soil: peering
Past the short tree that stands
In place for us, sawed-off, unbendable: a thing
Pile-driven down
And flowering from the impact—such weaving
Consuming delicacy in the leaves, out of such
Up-wedged and pineappled bark! We look alive
Through those petals in the censer-swung pots: through
That swinging soil, and the split leaves fountaining out
Of the mauled tree, to the east horizon vibrant
With whole-earth hold-down, past a single sail pillowing
From there on out.

We peer also from the flat
Slant sand, west from estuary-glitter,
From the reed-beds bending inland
At dawn as we do, to the high-ground hard-hurdling
Power of the down-mountain torrent: at a blue-ridged glance
From the ocean, we see all we have
Is unified as a quilt: the long leaves of the short tree,
The tough churchly feathers, dance rice-like this side of
The far-out wave-break's lounging
Curved insolent long sparking thorn, and
The gull's involving balance, his sweeping-through shuttle-run
Downwind; his tapestry-move
Is laid on our shoulders, where the unspilled dead
Are riding, wild with flowers, collision-colors
At the hairline, tended, sufficient, dead-level with us
From now on out.

What visions to us from all this lived
Humidity? What insights from blue haze alone? From kudzu?
From snake-vine? From the native dog-sized deer

From island to island floating, their head-bones
Eternal and formal,
Collisionless? We are standing mainly on blends
Of sand, red-rooted, in dark
Near-fever air, and there is a certain weaving
At our backs, like a gull's over-the-shoulder
Peel-off downwind. Assuming those wings, we keep gazing
From goat-grass to the high
Shifts, splits, and barreling
Alcohol of the rocks, all the way from minnows flashing whole
The bright brittle shallows, waiting for our momentum
From here on out.

It is true, we like our air warm
And wild, and the bark of our trees
Overlapping backward and upward
Stoutly, the shocks of tough leaves counter-
balancing, with a flicker of lostness. Beside the dead,
The straw-sucking marsh, we have stood where every blade
Of eelgrass thrilled like a hand-line
For the huge bass hanging in the shade
Of the sunken bush, and have heard the unstuffed moss
Hiss like a laundry-iron. This point between
The baskets and the tree is where we best
Are, and would be: our soil, our soul,
Our sail, our black horizon simmering like a mainspring,
Our rocky water falling like a mountain
Ledge-to-ledge naturally headlong,
Unstoppable, and our momentum
In place, overcoming, coming over us
And from us
from now on out.

Vessels

When the sound of forest leaves is like the sleep-talk
Of half-brothers; when it trembles   shorts itself out
Between branches, and is like light that does not cost
Itself any light, let me turn: turn right thén,

Right as it happens and say: I crave wandering
And giving: I crave

My own blood, that makes the body
Of the lover in my arms give up
On the great sparking vault of her form,
when I think instead
Of my real brother, who talks like no leaf
Or no half,
and of the road he will be on
As my body drops off
And the step he takes from me
Comes kicking,
and he feels the starry head that has hovered

Above him all his life

come down on his, like mine

Exactly,

or near enough.

Sleepers

There is a sound you can make, as if someone asked you
To sing between oar strokes, or as though
Your birth-cry came back, and you put it into sails
Over water,
                        or without vocal cords, like a torso,
Said what it meant, regardless. That is the voice
For sleepers; find it—
Use it and you can join them, that assault-force

Without a muscle, fighting for space

To lift in planned rows over graveyards
Like full battalions. Not one can give you the location
Of his stump-stillness, or even one

Of his edges; none knows where his body will end,
Or what it is stamped with
This moment: agate,

Nova-burst   earthworm
Owl feather.
                        Sound off, sleepers,
Headless singers. One.
                                One, two: Sound off.
Not knowing where your tombs
Already lie, assemble, sail through

The lifted spaces, unburied.

Meadow Bridge

There might be working some kind of throwaway

Meditation on Being, just
From what I am looking at
Right here. I can't tell, myself. But it may already have happened
When I batted my eye—

a new fix

Of sun lined out, squaring off: a fresh
Steel bridge,
exactly true
To a crosscut of starkness
And silver.
Tell me: why do I want
To put over it, the right hand drawing

Inexhaustibly drawing
out of the left, a vibration

Of threads? This also, beholders,
Is a fact: gauze
Burns off,
keeps coming: the bridge breaks through anything
I can pull from my hand. No matter how I brim, there is

No softening.

Field, what hope?

Tomb Stone

This place named you,
And what business I have here
Is what I think it is
And only that. I must ask you, though, not to fall

Any farther,
               and to forgive me
For coming here, as I keep doing,
                       as I have done
For a while in a vertical body
That breathes the rectangular solitude

Risen over you. I want time to tell the others
Not to come, for I understand

Now, that deep enough
In death, the earth becomes
Absolute earth. Hold all there is: hold on
And forgive, while I tell them as I tell
Myself where I stand: Don't let a breast

Echo, because of a foot.

                    Pass, human step.

To Be Done in Winter

in memoriam, T. C.

What you hold,
Don't drink it all. Throw what you have left of it
Out, and stand. Where the drink went away
Rejoice that your fingers are burning
Like hammered snow.

He makes no sound: the cold flurries, and he comes all the way
Back into life; in the mind
There is no decay. Imagine him
As to behold him, for if you fail
To remember, he lies without
What his body was.

His short shadow
Is on you. Bring him in, now, with tools
And elements. Behold him

With your arms: encircle him,
Bring him in with the forge and the crystal,

With the spark-pounding cold.

Moon Flock

No, don't ask me to give you
What happened in my head when the dark felt
It should change: when the black ploughblade
Went through and dissolved. That was bad enough,

But if you want to understand

Frustration, look up while the moon, which is nothing

But a wild white world,

Struggles overhead: fights to grow wings
For its creatures but cannot get
Creatures to have them. It is known: nothing can be put

Up on a wind with no air;
No wing can lift from stones
Lighter than earth-stones, where a man could leap

Leap till he's nearly forever

Overhead: overhead floating.

No wings,
In all that lightness. You want to understand:

All right. You don't have to look up, but can look straight

Straight

Straight out   out over the night sea
As it comes in. Do that.
Do it and think of your death, too, as a white world

Struggling for wings. Then
All the water your eyesight will hold
While it can, will not be lost

And neither will the moon
As it strains and does nothing
But quiver
             when the whole earth places you
        Underfoot
                   as though suspended
For good. You deserve it. Yóu should be

That moon flock; and not, as you wíll be,
A moveless man floating in the earth

As though overhead, where it is not
Possible to wave your arms
At something, or at nothing: at a white world

Or at your mother, or at the ocean
In shock, that I told you about, all insanity
And necessity when it sees you, and is right at you

        Coming
                hair-tearing

Hair-tearing and coming.

Snow Thickets

Helplessly besieging: it is dim,

Unity wavering

Wavering on us, the land in cancelling flak. From inside, you and I
Are watching gravity come down

In monotonous awe
                               each flake a part

Of it, or not. With no blinking, we do

As the snow does

                eyes burning   thorns hooding   our tongues

Being born: we watch, under the bush

Being bound, those all-whites yearning
For anvil-points, for contact,
                            still holding
The airborne embattlement:

Offered and cutthroat   lost
Very great winning hand

Down-dealt to the upthrust.

Expanses

Enjoyable clouds, and a man comes;

It's true, he's alive, but from this distance
No one could tell he is breathing.
You want to be sure he knows, though,
Not to confuse the sea
With any kind of heart: never to mix blood with something

As free as foam. The color white is wing, water, cloud;
It is best as sail.

Sail.

Drawn always off, off the sea
To the chopped soft road, your look
Goes willingly yonder, to and through
The far friendly mountain

then

Back over earth level-jawed   shoulder-energy widening
From water, everywhere there is land,

Brother: boundless,
Earthbound, trouble-free, and all you want—

Joy like short grass.

Double-tongue

Collaborations and Rewrites

Lakes of Värmland

with André Frénaud

Under the terrible north-light north-sea
Light blue: severe smile of a warrior who sleeps in chain-mail
Like a child: sleeps for the many, in water turned to brass
By the dumped cannon of Charles the Twelfth—
                                        leave them at their level,
            O Sweden, like the ultimate weapons,
   Like the last war-dead
                    steeped in the angles of your just light—

A single pine tree standing for my heart, I wish to gather near them
        Anything that grows; myrtle, this stuff could be,

        Or bilberry; whatever.

Form

with André Frénaud

I

Pull out the pissed-on clinkers,
Rake down the ashes of my bed, and come in

And let's do it, as cold as we can get,

Calving into the void like glaciers
Into the green Northern Sea. Give me a cliff-shudder
When you're finishing, before you split off
Unheard, almost booming: cliff-shudder   child-shudder

That ends it. We have been here before, as you know.

II

We have been here again, humped-up and splintering
Like ice-junk: here it has happened
But we missed it, and dead birds from many migrations
Float eye-up between us,
                                    between bergs, Carrara-piles

Where we chopped and hacked, shattering glass, searching jaggedly
For the radiant nude ice-sculpture
That never showed   never shaped itself free

                    Of us   was never anything
But chip-chaff and gentian-blue zero
                                              and, as before,
The glorious being we froze together
To bring forth, that we chiseled toward closer and closer,
Whinging and ringing, weeping

For discovery: that together we have annihilated
But not found, is now no more

Than our two hostile cadavers, together.

Heads

with Lucien Becker

I

There is no longer any reason to confuse
My breath with the room's. Sleep empties the pillow;
The world looks into various windows
Where human beings are unfinished,

Like blueprints; no substance has come.
Meadow-saffron dries, tenses. Morning pulverizes it
With a single vague foot, heavy as with
All the sleepless eyelids that there are.

The wellsprings are gray as the sky;
The smoky wind, a wind for headless people,
Flees with the thousands of voices
That solitude waits for, like tide-slack.

Above the roofs everything is empty;
Light cannot get all the way up
To where it was, stalled in dim lamp-bulbs
And bottles drunk dry to hold it down.

II

Beyond the sill the day has started and quit.
The sheet has cut off my head; my mirror's
Still deep with the whole night,
And the road has made great progress

Into the wall. A fly goes all around
In a big balance. I used to lie here, darling,
With unimproved light: I took it from your brow
To mine, a glimmer over well-springs,

Not zoned, not floor-planned for death.
But a building you can see through is rising:
They are settling and dressing the stones
That pain from everywhere, so long as human,

Fastens onto like clothespins. Lie still, though;
We're not hanging. You are always covered
By your smooth forehead and your eyelids;
You are grazed by no tissued humming

Of razor wire, or by the shadows that come out
Framing, scraping, hosing-down sides of glass,
And leave for a specified time
The sides of their heads against banks.

Farmers

a fragment
with André Frénaud

There are not many meteors over the flat country

Of the old; not one metaphor between the ploughblade
  And the dirt
                not much for the spirit: not enough
        To raise the eyes past the horizon-line
  Even to the Lord, even with neck-muscles like a bull's
      For the up-toss. The modest face has no fear

        Of following a center-split swaying track
            Through grain and straw
        To the grave, or of the honor of work
  With muck and animals, as a man born reconciled
            With his dead kin:

When love gives him back the rough red of his face he dares

To true-up the seasons of life with the raggedness of earth,
    With the underground stream as it turns its water
  Into the free stand of the well: a language takes hold

        And keeps on, barely making it, made
    By pain: the pain that's had him ever since school,
      At the same time the indivisible common good
            Being shared among the family
      Came clear to him: he disappears into fog

        He reappears he forces out his voice

        Over the field   he extends his figures

          With a dead-right clumsiness,
        And the blazon that changes every year
  Its yellow and green squares, announces at each moment

What must be said: the justice that the power of man installs
In exhausted fresh-air coupling with the earth:
                                        Slogger—

                        Figure of glory

                Less and more than real, fooled always
            By the unforeseeable: so nailed by your steps
Into the same steps   so marked by wisdom calamitously come by,
                And always uncertain, valiantly balancing,
            So stripped, so hog-poor still, after a long day
                In the immemorial, that I cannot say to you
                        Where you will hear me,
                Farmer, there will be no end to your knowing

                The pastures drawn breathless by the furrow,
            The fields, heartsick, unquenchable   arid
                                                avid,
            The forgivable slowness, the whispered prophecies of weather:
                Winter   spring, the season that always comes through
                        For you, and never enough,

                        But only dies, turning out
                    In its fragile green, its rich greens,
                To be nothing but the great stain of blankness
                        Changing again—

                            Gravedigger

            On Sunday, you come back Monday to the laying-out
        In squares, of your infinite land
                                the furs of snow do not reach us
            When they should
                        the moon has troubled the sown seed . . .

Craters

with Michel Leiris

Roots out of the ground and ongoing
The way we are, some of them—

Spokes   earth-slats   a raft made of humped planks
Slung down and that's right: wired together
By the horizon: it's what *these* roads
Are growing through: fatal roads,
No encounters, the hacked grass burning with battle-song—

Then when we get *our* voices together,
When we mix in that savage way, in the gully of throats
Where the fog piles up, and we turn our long cadences loose
Over the grooved pasture, the running fence of song

Will flap and mount straight up for miles

Very high, all staring stridulation,
Softer than beer-hops:

one of the days when the wind breathes slackly,
Making the lightest perches tremble
Like hostile stems interlacing,
As in the heart a lock of blond hair knots on itself
Suicidally, insolubly
someone will plough-out a door,
A staircase will dig itself down, its haunted spiral

Will blacken and come out

Where the ashes of those who were once turned to Pompeian lava
Will abandon their smouldering silkworks,
Their velvet slags, and take on the courtliness
Of ghosts: then, then the sky will be gone from us

Forever, we wretched ones who can love nothing
But light.
              Such will the craters tell you—any crater
Will tell you, dry-heaving and crouching:
                              will tell us we've stumbled
Onto one:
          we're in one, dry-heaving and crouching.

Attempted Departure

with André du Bouchet

I come back

hoping to leave

From these planks; for farewell and for lift-off I am lighting
Four walls of a fire, here. Blank plaster comes alive
On me in square gold: my shadow goes giddy with dimension, dropping off
The outflanked pious hunger of the flat;
The damn thing can come at me now
Like death, from anywhere

but while I stand
No side protected, at home, play-penned
With holocaust
the slashes disappear from this flayed back, like
My step on the rammed road,

the only thing fleeing.

Poem

through a French poet, Roland Bouhéret, and my running father

For having left the birds that left me
Better streaks on my eyes than they can make
On any sky alive:
                    for having broken loose new stars
By opening to the storm a deaf window

At the moment the summer park closed:
                            for having rubbed out,
From cliffs not dangerous enough, or cold enough
            For you,
                    the name of the dead,
I hear the sound of fresh steps seeding toward me,
            Steps I could take.

                    Gene,

            Dead in the full of July
Ten years ago, I have learned all the tracks
Of the stars of that month: they give me more body-authority
Than a beast-birth in straw. Believe me I have kept

The old river that ran like something from a crock,
Through the cow-battered weeds: that runs over us
            As baptismal water always;
            I believe I could be walking there

            Like high valleys crossing,
In the long laconic open-striding fullness

Of your muscular death. In whole air your form
Takes up with me best, giving more than it could
            In the hospital's mirror-blanked room
Where you leaned toward the grim parks under you

    Before they closed,
                    and out of the rattling rails

Of your cocked bed, talked about mowing, nothing
But mowing, of all weird, unearthly
Earthly things: like a shower of grassblades
Talked, tilted and talked,
                              and shivered, down past you, the gaunt
Traffic-islands into green; from that time on, I saw them
As blocked fields, part of elsewhere.

                                        But we are advancing
By steps that grew back to my door,
And if I set your long name in the wind
And it comes back spelling out
The name of a far port-of-call,
                                  the place we never got to,
That is all right.
                        And yet, with the ashy river
Running like a soul where I'm headed,
Even with the names of harbors that swarmed all over me
When I hit the open, when I paced myself exactly
With the current—these and the birds, the old cows,

Have stubborned here
                          stalled   no matter how I increase
My leg-beat, or stretch and find myself
Calling out in mid-stride. You are motionless, you are in the middle
Of elsewhere, breathing the herd-breath
Of the dead—singled and in-line breathing

Among so many—looking in the same direction
As the rest of them, your long legs covered with burrs
And bent weeds, splinters of grassblades:
Squared-off, power-bodied, pollen-lidded

You are: green-leggèd, but nailed there.

Purgation

homage, Po Chü-yi

Before and after the eye, grasses go over the long fields.
Every season they walk on
      by us, as though—no; I and you,
  Dear friend—decreed it. One time or another

 They are here. Grass season . . . yet we are no longer the best
   Of us.
     Lie stiller, closer; in the April I love

 For its juices, there is too much green for your grave.
  I feel that the Spring should ignite with what is
Unnatural as we; ours, but God-suspected. It should come in one furious step, and leave
Some—a little—green for us; never quite get every one of the hummocks tremoring vaguely

 Tall in the passed-through air. They'd make the old road *be*
 The road for old men, where you and I used to wander toward
 The beetle-eaten city gate, as the year leaned into us.
   Oh fire, come *on*! I trust you!

 My ancient human friend, you are dead, as we both know.

 But I remember, and I call for something serious, uncalled-for
By anyone else, to sweep, to *use*
    the dryness we've caused to become us! Like the grasshopper

 I speak, nearly covered with dust, from the footprint and ask
Not for the line-squall lightning:
      the cloud's faking veins—Yes! I catch myself:
  No; not the ripped cloud's open touch the fireball hay
   Of August
      but for flame too old to live
  Or die, to travel like a wide wild contrary
  Single-minded brow over the year's right growing
 In April
    over us *for us* as we sway stubbornly near death
    From both sides age-gazing

 Both sighing like grass and fire.

Basics

I. Level

Who has told you what discoveries
There are, along the stressed blank
Of a median line? From it, nothing

Can finally fall. Like a spellbinder's pass
A tense placid principle continues

Over it, and when you follow you have the drift,

The balance of many compass needles
Verging to the pole. *Bring down your arms, voyager,*

And the soul goes out
Surrounding, humming
standing by means

Of the match-up in long arm-bones

Dropped:
held out and drawn back   back in
Out of the open
compass-quivering and verging
At your sides, as median movement

Lays itself bare: a closed vein of bisected marble, where

Along the hairline stem
Of the continuum, you progress, trembling
With the plumb-bob quiver of mid-earth,
with others in joy
Moving also, in line,

Equalling, armlessing.

II. Simplex

Comes a single thread
>   monofilament coming

Strengthening   engrossing and slitting
Into the fine-spun life

To come, foretold in whatever
Ecstasy there's been, but never suspected, never included
In what was believed. The balance of the spiral
Had been waiting, and could take

What was given it: the single upthrust through
The hanging acid, the helix spun and spellbound

By the God-set of chemistry, the twine much deeper
Than any two bodies imagined
They could die for: insinuate, woven
Single strand, third serpent
Of the medical wood, circling the staff of life

Into the very body

Of the future, deadly
But family, having known from the beginning

Of the sun, what will take it on.

III. Word

Heat makes this, heat makes any
Word: human lungs,
Human lips. Not like eternity, which, naked, every time
Will call on lightning
To say it all: No after
Or before. We try for that

And fail. Our voice
Fails, but for an instant
Is like the other; breath alone
That came as though humanly panting
From far back, in unspeakably beautiful

Empty space

And struck: at just this moment
Found the word "golden."

About the Author

James Dickey was born in Atlanta, Georgia. He received his B.A. (1949) and M.A. (1950) from Vanderbilt University in between two military stints, in the U.S. Army Air Force during the Second World War and in the U.S. Air Force during the Korean War. Dickey's previous books with Wesleyan include *Drowning with Others* (1962), *Helmets* (1962), *Buck-dancer's Choice* (1965), *Falling, May Day Sermon, and Other Poems* (1981), *The Early Motion* (1982), and *The Central Motion: Poems 1968–1979* (1983). Dickey has received many awards including a Guggenheim Fellowship, a National Book Award and Melville Cane Award for *Buck-dancer's Choice*, and the French Prix Médicis for his novel *Deliverance*. He is a member of the National Institute of Arts and Letters, a fellow of the American Academy of Arts and Sciences, and in 1989 he was named judge for the Yale Series of Younger Poets. James Dickey is Carolina Professor and Poet-in-Residence at the University of South Carolina and lives in Columbia.

About the Book

The Eagle's Mile was composed on the Mergenthaler 202 in Sabon, a contemporary typeface based on classical prototypes. It was designed in 1964 by Jan Tschichold and based on the original types of Claude Garamond. This excellent typeface with gracefully bracketed serifs is perfectly suited to book composition. *The Eagle's Mile* was composed by Marathon Typography Service, Inc., Durham, North Carolina, and designed and produced by Kachergis Book Design, Pittsboro, North Carolina.

Wesleyan Poetry